BIRD VIEWING AREAS

1. Great Rann of Kutch
2. Thattekad Bird Sanctuary
3. Keoladeo National Park
4. Lava and Neora Valley
5. Kaziranga National Park & Eaglenest Wildlife Sanctuary
6. Corbett National Park
7. Bannerghatta National Park
8. Ranganathittu Bird Sanctuary
9. Nagarhole National Park
10. Dibru Saikhowa National Park
11. National Chambal Sanctuary
12. Blue Mountain National Park
13. The Desert National Park
14. Great Himalayan National Park
15. Point Calimere
16. Vembanad Wetland
17. Wular Lake
18. Gorumara National Park
19. Okhla Bird Sanctuary
20. Goa
21. Indira Gandhi National Park
22. Andaman Islands
23. Vedanthangal Bird Sanctuary
24. Pong Dam Wetlands

WILDLIFE SOS
INDIA

Researched by Wildlife SOS India. Most illustrations show the adult male in breeding coloration. Colors and markings may be duller or absent during different seasons. The measurements denote the length of species from bill to tail tip. Illustrations are not to scale.

Waterford Press produces reference guides that introduce novices to nature, science, survival and outdoor recreation. Product information is featured on the website:
www.waterfordpress.com
To order, call 800-434-2555.
For permissions, or to share comments, e-mail editor@waterfordpress.com For information on custom-published products, call 800-434-2555 or e-mail info@waterfordpress.com

Text and illustrations © 2015, 2021 by Waterford Press Inc. All rights reserved.
Cover images © Shutterstock.
Ecoregion map © The National Atlas of the United States.

$7.95 U.S.
ISBN 978-1-58355-939-0

211529
Made in the USA

INDIA BIRDS

A Folding Pocket Guide to Familiar Species

INDIA BIRDS – A Folding Pocket Guide to Familiar Species

Kavanagh/Leung

T0123924

Little Grebe
Tachybaptus ruficollis
To 30 cm (12 in.)
Also called dabchick.

Common Teal
Anas crecca To 40 cm (16 in.)
Widespread winter visitor.

Northern Shoveler
Spatula clypeata To 50 cm (20 in.)
Named for its large spatulate bill.
Widespread winter visitor.

Mallard
Anas platyrhynchos To 70 cm (28 in.)
Widespread winter visitor.

Northern Pintail
Anas acuta To 75 cm (30 in.)
Widespread winter visitor.

Spot-billed Duck
Anas poecilorhyncha
To 63 cm (25 in.)
Bill has a yellow tip.

Knob-billed Duck
Sarkidiornis melanotos
To 75 cm (30 in.)
Also called comb duck.

Greylag Goose
Anser anser
To 83 cm (33 in.)
Widespread winter visitor.

Oriental Dwarf Kingfisher
Ceyx erithaca
To 13 cm (5 in.)

Common Kingfisher
Alcedo atthis
To 18 cm (7 in.)

White-throated Kingfisher
Halcyon smyrnensis
To 28 cm (11 in.)

Pied Kingfisher
Ceryle rudis
To 25 cm (10 in.)

Common Snipe
Gallinago gallinago
To 30 cm (12 in.)
Widespread winter visitor.

Ruddy Turnstone
Arenaria interpres
To 25 cm (10 in.)

Eurasian Curlew
Numenius arquata
To 63 cm (25 in.)
Widespread winter visitor.

Little Ringed Plover
Charadrius dubius
To 15 cm (6 in.)

Red-wattled Lapwing
Vanellus indicus
To 35 cm (14 in.)
Red bill has a black tip.

Black-winged Stilt
Himantopus himantopus
To 38 cm (15 in.)

Eurasian Thick-knee
Burhinus oedicnemus
To 43 cm (17 in.)
Note large eyes.

Black-headed Gull
Chroicocephalus ridibundus
To 38 cm (15 in.)

Pied Avocet
Recurvirostra avosetta
To 45 cm (18 in.)

Indian Skimmer
Rynchops albicollis
To 40 cm (16 in.)
Feeds by skimming over water with its lower bill cutting the water's surface to spear fish.

River Tern
Sterna aurantia
To 45 cm (18 in.)

Caspian Tern
Hydroprogne caspia
To 60 cm (2 ft.)

Pheasant-tailed Jacana
Hydrophasianus chirurgus
To 58 cm (23 in.)

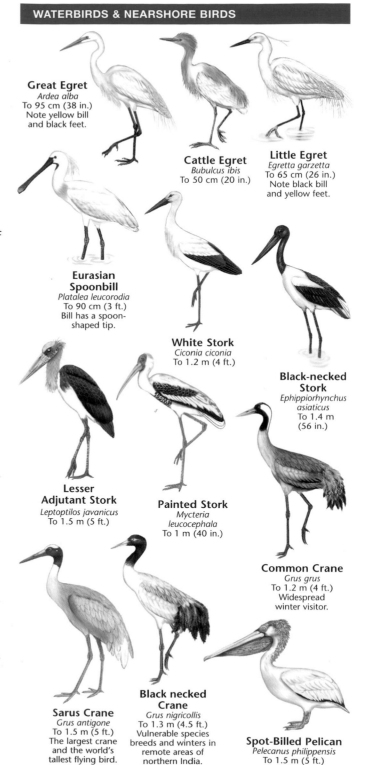

Great Egret
Ardea alba
To 95 cm (38 in.)
Note yellow bill and black feet.

Cattle Egret
Bubulcus ibis
To 50 cm (20 in.)

Little Egret
Egretta garzetta
To 65 cm (26 in.)
Note black bill and yellow feet.

Eurasian Spoonbill
Platalea leucorodia
To 90 cm (3 ft.)
Bill has a spoon-shaped tip.

White Stork
Ciconia ciconia
To 1.2 m (4 ft.)

Black-necked Stork
Ephippiorhynchus asiaticus
To 1.4 m (56 in.)

Lesser Adjutant Stork
Leptoptilos javanicus
To 1.5 m (5 ft.)

Painted Stork
Mycteria leucocephala
To 1 m (40 in.)

Common Crane
Grus grus
To 1.2 m (4 ft.)
Widespread winter visitor.

Sarus Crane
Grus antigone
To 1.5 m (5 ft.)
The largest crane and the world's tallest flying bird.

Black necked Crane
Grus nigricollis
To 1.3 m (4.5 ft.)
Vulnerable species breeds and winters in remote areas of northern India.

Spot-Billed Pelican
Pelecanus philippensis
To 1.5 m (5 ft.)

Purple Heron
Ardea purpurea
To 90 cm (3 ft.)

Black-crowned Night-Heron
Nycticorax nycticorax
To 70 cm (28 in.)

Grey Heron
Ardea cinerea
To 95 cm (38 in.)

Indian Pond Heron
Ardeola grayii
To 45 cm (18 in.)

Little Cormorant
Microcarbo niger
To 50 cm (20 in.)

Great Cormorant
Phalacrocorax carbo
To 1 m (40 in.)
Note white throat patch.

Little Heron
Butorides striatus
To 35 cm (14 in.)
Note black cap.

Common Gallinule
Gallinula galeata
To 35 cm (14 in.)

Greater Flamingo
Phoenicopterus ruber
To 1.2 m (4 ft.)

Purple Swamphen
Porphyrio porphyrio
To 45 cm (18 in.)

Indian Darter
Anhinga melanogaster
To 1 m (40 in.)
Note long, slender neck and pointed yellowish bill.

Eurasian Coot
Fulica atra
To 40 cm (16 in.)

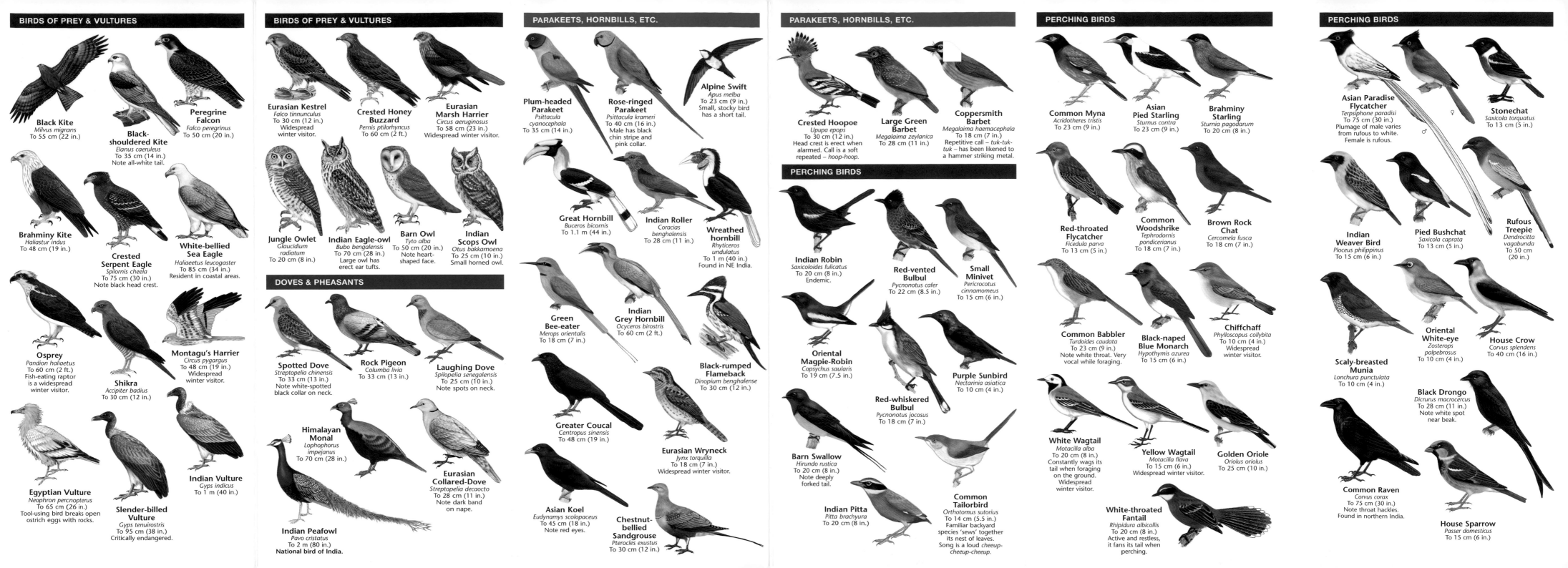

BIRDS OF PREY & VULTURES

Black Kite
Milvus migrans
To 55 cm (22 in.)

Black-shouldered Kite
Elanus caeruleus
To 35 cm (14 in.)
Note all-white tail.

Peregrine Falcon
Falco peregrinus
To 50 cm (20 in.)

Brahminy Kite
Haliastur indus
To 48 cm (19 in.)

Crested Serpent Eagle
Spilornis cheela
To 75 cm (30 in.)
Note black head crest.

White-bellied Sea Eagle
Haliaeetus leucogaster
To 85 cm (34 in.)
Resident in coastal areas.

Osprey
Pandion haliaetus
To 60 cm (2 ft.)
Fish-eating raptor is a widespread winter visitor.

Shikra
Accipiter badius
To 30 cm (12 in.)

Montagu's Harrier
Circus pygargus
To 48 cm (19 in.)
Widespread winter visitor.

Egyptian Vulture
Neophron percnopterus
To 65 cm (26 in.)
Tool-using bird breaks open ostrich eggs with rocks.

Slender-billed Vulture
Gyps tenuirostris
To 95 cm (38 in.)
Critically endangered.

Indian Vulture
Gyps indicus
To 1 m (40 in.)

BIRDS OF PREY & VULTURES

Eurasian Kestrel
Falco tinnunculus
To 30 cm (12 in.)
Widespread winter visitor.

Crested Honey Buzzard
Pernis ptilorhyncus
To 60 cm (2 ft.)

Eurasian Marsh Harrier
Circus aeruginosus
To 58 cm (23 in.)
Widespread winter visitor.

Jungle Owlet
Glaucidium radiatum
To 20 cm (8 in.)

Indian Eagle-owl
Bubo bengalensis
To 70 cm (28 in.)
Large owl has erect ear tufts.

Barn Owl
Tyto alba
To 50 cm (20 in.)
Note heart-shaped face.

Indian Scops Owl
Otus bakkamoena
To 25 cm (10 in.)
Small horned owl.

DOVES & PHEASANTS

Spotted Dove
Streptopelia chinensis
To 33 cm (13 in.)
Note white-spotted black collar on neck.

Rock Pigeon
Columba livia
To 33 cm (13 in.)

Laughing Dove
Spilopelia senegalensis
To 25 cm (10 in.)
Note spots on neck.

Himalayan Monal
Lophophorus impejanus
To 70 cm (28 in.)

Eurasian Collared-Dove
Streptopelia decaocto
To 28 cm (11 in.)
Note dark band on nape.

Indian Peafowl
Pavo cristatus
To 2 m (80 in.)
National bird of India.

PARAKEETS, HORNBILLS, ETC.

Plum-headed Parakeet
Psittacula cyanocephala
To 35 cm (14 in.)

Rose-ringed Parakeet
Psittacula krameri
To 40 cm (16 in.)
Male has black chin stripe and pink collar.

Alpine Swift
Apus melba
To 23 cm (9 in.)
Small, stocky bird has a short tail.

Great Hornbill
Buceros bicornis
To 1.1 m (44 in.)

Indian Roller
Coracias benghalensis
To 28 cm (11 in.)

Wreathed hornbill
Rhyticeros undulatus
To 1 m (40 in.)
Found in NE India.

Green Bee-eater
Merops orientalis
To 18 cm (7 in.)

Indian Grey Hornbill
Ocyceros birostris
To 60 cm (2 ft.)

Black-rumped Flameback
Dinopium benghalense
To 30 cm (12 in.)

Greater Coucal
Centropus sinensis
To 48 cm (19 in.)

Eurasian Wryneck
Jynx torquilla
To 18 cm (7 in.)
Widespread winter visitor.

Asian Koel
Eudynamys scolopaceus
To 45 cm (18 in.)
Note red eyes.

Chestnut-bellied Sandgrouse
Pterocles exustus
To 30 cm (12 in.)

PARAKEETS, HORNBILLS, ETC.

Crested Hoopoe
Upupa epops
To 30 cm (12 in.)
Head crest is erect when alarmed. Call is a soft repeated – *hoop-hoop*.

Large Green Barbet
Megalaima zeylanica
To 28 cm (11 in.)

Coppersmith Barbet
Megalaima haemacephala
To 18 cm (7 in.)
Repetitive call – *tuk-tuk-tuk* – has been likened to a hammer striking metal.

PERCHING BIRDS

Indian Robin
Saxicoloides fulicatus
To 20 cm (8 in.)
Endemic.

Red-vented Bulbul
Pycnonotus cafer
To 22 cm (8.5 in.)

Small Minivet
Pericrocotus cinnamomeus
To 15 cm (6 in.)

Oriental Magpie-Robin
Copsychus saularis
To 19 cm (7.5 in.)

Red-whiskered Bulbul
Pycnonotus jocosus
To 18 cm (7 in.)

Purple Sunbird
Nectarinia asiatica
To 10 cm (4 in.)

Barn Swallow
Hirundo rustica
To 20 cm (8 in.)
Note deeply forked tail.

Indian Pitta
Pitta brachyura
To 20 cm (8 in.)

Common Tailorbird
Orthotomus sutorius
To 14 cm (5.5 in.)
Familiar backyard species 'sews' together its nest of leaves. Song is a loud *cheeup-cheeup-cheeup*.

PERCHING BIRDS

Common Myna
Acridotheres tristis
To 23 cm (9 in.)

Asian Pied Starling
Sturnus contra
To 23 cm (9 in.)

Brahminy Starling
Sturnia pagodarum
To 20 cm (8 in.)

Red-throated Flycatcher
Ficedula parva
To 13 cm (5 in.)

Common Woodshrike
Tephrodornis pondicerianus
To 18 cm (7 in.)

Brown Rock Chat
Cercomela fusca
To 18 cm (7 in.)

Common Babbler
Turdoides caudata
To 23 cm (9 in.)
Note white throat. Very vocal while foraging.

Black-naped Blue Monarch
Hypothymis azurea
To 15 cm (6 in.)

Chiffchaff
Phylloscopus collybita
To 10 cm (4 in.)
Widespread winter visitor.

White Wagtail
Motacilla alba
To 20 cm (8 in.)
Constantly wags its tail when foraging on the ground. Widespread winter visitor.

Yellow Wagtail
Motacilla flava
To 15 cm (6 in.)
Widespread winter visitor.

Golden Oriole
Oriolus oriolus
To 25 cm (10 in.)

White-throated Fantail
Rhipidura albicollis
To 20 cm (8 in.)
Active and restless, it fans its tail when perching.

PERCHING BIRDS

Asian Paradise Flycatcher
Terpsiphone paradisi
To 75 cm (30 in.)
Plumage of male varies from rufous to white. Female is rufous.

Stonechat
Saxicola torquatus
To 13 cm (5 in.)

Indian Weaver Bird
Ploceus philippinus
To 15 cm (6 in.)

Pied Bushchat
Saxicola caprata
To 13 cm (5 in.)

Rufous Treepie
Dendrocitta vagabunda
To 50 cm (20 in.)

Oriental White-eye
Zosterops palpebrosus
To 10 cm (4 in.)

House Crow
Corvus splendens
To 40 cm (16 in.)

Scaly-breasted Munia
Lonchura punctulata
To 10 cm (4 in.)

Black Drongo
Dicrurus macrocercus
To 28 cm (11 in.)
Note white spot near beak.

Common Raven
Corvus corax
To 75 cm (30 in.)
Note throat hackles. Found in northern India.

House Sparrow
Passer domesticus
To 15 cm (6 in.)